D1606614

HOW TO BECOME AN

ACCIDENTAL ENTREPRENEUR

HOW TO BECOME AN

ACCIDENTAL ENTREPRENEUR

Elizabeth MacLeod &
Frieda Wishinsky

illustrated by
Jenn Playford

ORCA BOOK PUBLISHERS

Text copyright © Elizabeth MacLeod and Frieda Wishinsky 2022
Illustrations copyright © Jenn Playford 2022

Published in Canada and the United States in 2022 by Orca Book Publishers.
orcabook.com

All rights reserved. No part of this publication may be reproduced or transmitted in any form or by any means, electronic or mechanical, including photocopying, recording or by any information storage and retrieval system now known or to be invented, without permission in writing from the publisher.

Library and Archives Canada Cataloguing in Publication

Title: How to become an accidental entrepreneur / Elizabeth MacLeod & Frieda Wishinsky ; illustrated by Jenn Playford.
Names: MacLeod, Elizabeth, author. | Wishinsky, Frieda, author. | Playford, Jenn, illustrator.
Description: Series statement: Accidental series ; 3 | Includes bibliographical references and index.
Identifiers: Canadiana (print) 20210352728 | Canadiana (ebook) 20210352736 | ISBN 9781459828339 (hardcover) | ISBN 9781459828346 (PDF) | ISBN 9781459828353 (EPUB)
Subjects: LCSH: Entrepreneurship—Juvenile literature. | LCSH: Businesspeople—Juvenile literature.
Classification: LCC HB615 .M33 2022 | DDC j338/.04—dc23

Library of Congress Control Number: 2021948729

Summary: This nonfiction book for middle-grade readers is full of stories of inspiring entrepreneurs, young and old, who have changed the world.

Orca Book Publishers is committed to reducing the consumption of nonrenewable resources in the production of our books. We make every effort to use materials that support a sustainable future.

Orca Book Publishers gratefully acknowledges the support for its publishing programs provided by the following agencies: the Government of Canada, the Canada Council for the Arts and the Province of British Columbia through the BC Arts Council and the Book Publishing Tax Credit.

The authors and publisher have made every effort to ensure that the information in this book was correct at the time of publication. The authors and publisher do not assume any liability for any loss, damage or disruption caused by errors or omissions. Every effort has been made to trace copyright holders and to obtain their permission for the use of copyrighted material. The publisher apologizes for any errors or omissions and would be grateful if notified of any corrections that should be incorporated in future reprints or editions of this book.

Cover and interior illustrations by Jenn Playford
Edited by Kirstie Hudson

Printed and bound in South Korea.

25 24 23 22 • 1 2 3 4

To my dear goddaughter Isabel, with love from Auntie Amy. May your budding entrepreneurial spirit of ingenuity, curiosity and intuitive know-how continue to flourish and build in you a strong sense of purpose and decisive action that leads to fulfillment for you and those around you.
—E.M.

For my friend Elisabeth Neumann.
—F.W.

CONTENTS

INTRODUCTION

Why do you start a new business?

Where do entrepreneurs get their ideas?

How do they make their businesses thrive?

What drives some entrepreneurs to use their ability and wealth to help others pursue their dreams and lead better lives?

In *How to Become an Accidental Entrepreneur*, we tell the fascinating stories of entrepreneurs who didn't plan on starting a new business but succeeded when they did.

> "A goal without a plan is just a wish."
>
> —Antoine de Saint-Exupéry, aviator and author of *The Little Prince*

The story of each entrepreneur is unique, but many share qualities that have helped them achieve success.

Each entrepreneur has faced obstacles—some have confronted prejudice because of their race, gender or age. Some have had to overcome poverty. Most have found it challenging to introduce a new idea and turn it into a business.

These women and men come from diverse backgrounds and different countries. But each entrepreneur learned from other people's experiences. Each studied, listened and was open to change. Each knew their strengths and learned from their mistakes.

The truth is that entrepreneurs don't succeed all on their own. They need mentors, support and co-workers.

Perhaps you'd like to start a business one day. Perhaps you'd like to do something that changes lives for the better, helps the environment and makes our planet safer for everyone.

Reading about entrepreneurs and noting how they accomplished their goals can guide a new entrepreneur on the road to success.

That entrepreneur might be you!

JERRY

BEN

Fariel Salahuddin

SPANX

SARA BLAKELY

CHAPTER ONE
BE OPEN TO RISK

Shiza Shahid knew how dangerous it would be to work with Pakistani activist Malala Yousafzai, but that didn't prevent her from helping. From the time Shahid was a young woman, she'd taken risks working on projects close to her heart and beliefs.

At 14 she worked with women prisoners in Pakistan. When she saw a YouTube video of a young Yousafzai helping girls go to school in the Swat Valley, Shahid invited Yousafzai to the secret camp she had established to help young women stand up for their right to an education. And when Yousafzai was shot for speaking out on educating girls, Shahid hurried to her side.

Shahid also assisted Yousafzai in establishing a **nonprofit** organization called Malala Fund. She has continued empowering people as the founder of NOW Ventures, which encourages companies to help people in their home community through education and **social services**. She believes that companies that help others also promote their own success.

Successful entrepreneurs like Shahid are open to risk and willing to try something new, even if it fails. They know that when situations change, sometimes they need to change direction too.

Richard Branson loved coming up with and trying new ideas. Some of the ideas worked out. Others failed. But nothing has stopped Branson, not even dyslexia, a condition that makes it difficult for him to read. After leaving school in London, England, at age 16, he started a magazine called *Student*. Although this first attempt at business failed, he soon tried another idea—opening a **discount** record store he dubbed Virgin, because everyone involved was new to business.

Branson made mistakes running the store—some even got him in trouble with the law—but he learned from those mistakes. His next venture was a record company, Virgin Records. The success of that company led to others. Branson has since been involved with about 50 new and diverse businesses. He says, "You fail if you don't try," and he lives by those words.

MORE THAN ICE CREAM

Ben Cohen
(1951–)

and Jerry Greenfield
(1951–)

From the beginning, Ben Cohen and Jerry Greenfield had a lot in common. They were both born in the same year in Brooklyn. They became friends in junior high school, although they lost touch after graduating high school. Cohen went on to college but dropped out and drove an ice-cream truck while taking courses in art and pottery. When he couldn't get into medical school, Greenfield worked as a **lab technician**.

In 1977 the friends met again in Saratoga Springs, New York, and decided to follow their old dream of creating a food business. They took a **correspondence course** in ice-cream making from Pennsylvania State University. After graduating with A's, they headed to Burlington, Vermont, to open an ice-cream parlor. They had no idea if their risky new venture would work, but their creative ice-cream flavors, such as Chocolate Chip Cookie Dough and Chunky Monkey, plus their commitment to projects that help communities, contributed to their success.

By 1980 Ben and Jerry had expanded their ice-cream business to an old mill, where they invented more wild and tasty flavors. Soon their innovative approach to ice cream and community service landed them a cover story in *Time* magazine. A few years later they established the Ben & Jerry's Foundation to donate some of their profits to local organizations and charities. Their programs supported social justice, better access to housing, making health services available and combating poverty.

When the giant food company Pillsbury felt Ben & Jerry's was too much competition for its own ice-cream **brand**, Cohen and Greenfield fought back through a **media** campaign asking their customers to stand with them against the large corporation's bullying. It worked.

In 1997 they published a book called *Ben & Jerry's Double-Dip: Lead with Your Values and Make Money, Too.* Even though Cohen and Greenfield eventually sold their ice-cream company, they're still involved in community outreach, promoting justice and fairness.

GREAT IDEA!

My Favorite Ice Cream Is...
In ice-cream polls, chocolate and vanilla are usually people's favorite flavors. But for Ben & Jerry's ice-cream lovers, Half Baked, a mishmash of cookie dough and fudge brownies, is number one, followed by the cherry and fudge-flake deliciousness of Cherry Garcia (named after Jerry Garcia, lead guitarist of the Grateful Dead).

Ben Cohen and Jerry Greenfield, the founders of Ben & Jerry's, work to combat climate change.

LOOKING GOOD!

Sara Blakely

(1971–)

"Logic will get you from A to B. Imagination will take you everywhere."

—Albert Einstein,
Nobel Prize–winning scientist

Florida-born Sara Blakely wanted to be a trial lawyer like her dad, but she didn't do well in the LSAT, a test to get into law school.

What should she do next? Head to Walt Disney World in Orlando, of course! Blakely applied for a job playing Goofy, a favorite Disney character. When that didn't pan out, she found a job helping customers at the resort's Epcot Center and also worked part-time as a stand-up comedian.

When she'd had enough of that, Blakely left to sell **fax machines** door-to-door. "Most doors were slammed in my face," she recalls. Despite the challenges of that job, Blakely discovered that she was good at sales. The door-to-door work also convinced her that what she really wanted to do was create a product she cared about and run her own business selling it.

One day, getting ready for a party, Blakely cut the feet out of a pair of pantyhose in order to have a smooth look under her white pants. To her delight, she discovered she'd accidentally created something new and comfortable. That led to the invention of Spanx, invisible, tight-fitting undergarments.

Spanx was a hit! Introducing a new product is always risky, but consumers were ready for Blakely's concept. She worked hard, used her good sales skills and made Spanx a success. She attributes some of her drive to her father's influence. She notes that her father appreciated failure as long as you learned from it. "My father wanted us to try everything and feel free to push the envelope," she says.

Spanx can now be found in 50 countries. In 2012 *Forbes* magazine named Blakely the world's youngest self-made female billionaire.

As Blakely continues to run her company, she's also committed to giving half her wealth to charitable causes. She especially believes in empowering women and supporting small businesses.

GREAT IDEA!

Sending Information via Fax

What do companies consider when deciding what technology to use to transfer information? Privacy, familiarity and ease of use are important to many businesses. The fax machine, a tool for sending and receiving information, has been around for years, and although there are newer ways of transmitting information, many businesses in countries such as Germany and Japan still feel the fax machine meets their needs.

Sara Blakely's clothing ideas have expanded into attractive, successful stores.

IT'S ALL ABOUT GOATS

Fariel Salahuddin
(c. 1984–)

SUCCESS!

SCIENCE AND THE WORLD

Not only is Frances Arnold the first American woman to win a Nobel Prize in Chemistry, but she is also one of the few prize-winners who has been a part of starting three businesses. All three use science to solve real-world problems and help the environment. Arnold recognizes that new ventures are risky. "You learn on the job," she says. "There's no good class for being an entrepreneur. You do it, and not everything is going to be successful. It's painful when things are not successful, but that's part of the process."

After receiving a prestigious Fulbright **scholarship** and graduating from Columbia University's School of International and Public Affairs, Pakistani-born Fariel Salahuddin advised governments on how to provide energy by building power plants and how to use energy efficiently. But after visiting poor villages in Pakistan, she changed her focus. While speaking to local people, she realized that access to water was even more important than obtaining energy. Millions of people in Pakistan don't have access to clean water, and small, poor communities have an especially hard time getting enough water to meet their daily needs.

Many women have to walk for up to four hours to obtain water and carry it back to their community. It's backbreaking and difficult. But they have no choice. How could communities get water without buying expensive generators or counting on local women to haul it in from distant wells?

The answer came to Salahuddin when she realized that even in a poor community, most people owned goats.

What if they traded these goats for **solar-powered** water pumps? All they needed was someone to help organize the exchange. It was an unusual and risky idea, but Salahuddin was sure she could do it.

And that's how her organization Goats for Water, part of UpTrade, was born.

Salahuddin's goal was to help people help themselves with the resources they had at hand. UpTrade provided not only solar-powered water pumps but also fertilizer, lighting and other products needed by the community.

It also changed the way people interacted. When they brought their goats to trade for a pump or other item, they also exchanged ideas, stories and information. Salahuddin's idea continues to change lives, and she hopes to spread her idea to other parts of the world. So far her organization has reached 1,800 farmers.

Clean water is key to living a healthy life, but accessing it is difficult in many places around the world.

GREAT
IDEA!

Water Is Life!
All plants and animals need water to survive and thrive. Access to clean water is key to everyone on Earth. Today about a billion people do not have regular access to clean water.

CHAPTER TWO
SEIZE OPPORTUNITIES

Arlene Dickinson was struggling to make a living as a single mom when she joined a Calgary communications company in 1988. Ten years later she became owner of the company, thanks to her talent for **marketing**. By recognizing chances and grabbing them, Dickinson built the firm from a local company to one of Canada's biggest independent marketing and communication businesses.

With her company Arlene Dickinson Enterprises and as a co-star of the *Dragons' Den* television show, Dickinson encourages other entrepreneurs to seize opportunities. She's the national spokesperson for Breakfast Club of Canada, which makes sure kids get healthy meals to start the day.

Entrepreneurs excel at finding and taking advantage of openings that no one else sees. They can change direction when necessary and are constantly testing new concepts by asking, "Will it work?"

Even as a toddler in Japan, Sōichirō Honda was fascinated by cars. When he grew up, he started a company to make car parts for Toyota Motor Corporation. But one of Honda's factories was bombed in 1944, during World War II. The other collapsed the next year in an earthquake. So he seized the chance to make a change and started making motorized bicycles.

Honda's motorcycles became the bestselling motorcycles in the world, and the company later became known for cars, garden equipment, power generators and more. Honda loved car racing, and the company still sponsors many sports teams and events.

SUCCESS!

NEW TAKE ON OLD POTTERY

Angélica Moreno was working in an office in Puebla, Mexico, when she decided to take lessons to make Talavera pottery, a type of tin-enameled clay pottery that's been made in Spain since the 1500s.

In 1990 Moreno started her own pottery company, Talavera de la Reyna, named for a Spanish town. She hired graphic designers and painters to add innovative designs to the pottery. The works have been exhibited worldwide, and Moreno's company continues to expand.

SWEET-SMELLING SISTERS

Lynn-Marie Angus
(1984–)

and Melissa-Rae Angus
(1985–)

> "I never dreamed of success. I worked for it."
>
> —Estée Lauder,
> co-founder of cosmetics company bearing her name

While working in high-rise construction, Lynn-Marie Angus, whose ancestry is Gitxaala, Nisga'a, Cree and Métis, experienced racism and sexual harassment. Her sister, Melissa-Rae, was struggling to make a living in Vancouver, British Columbia.

Both sisters wanted to make a change, so they grabbed the chance to work together. They wanted their business to reflect their Indigenous heritage and promote growth and health. And the Angus sisters liked specialty bath bombs and soaps. In 2018 they started Sisters Sage, creating modern wellness and self-care products inspired by their culture.

Sisters Sage uses traditional ingredients such as cedar, sage, sweetgrass and tobacco. These are sacred plants used in Gitxaala and Nisga'a smudging ceremonies. The ceremony involves burning the plants to create smoke for purifying or clearing negative energy in a person or place. The Angus sisters also care for the earth by using **biodegradable** packaging on their products.

The bath bombs, salves, smokeless smudge spray and soaps sold by Sisters Sage are meaningful products to the Anguses, allowing them to share their Indigenous culture. As well, the sisters strive to inspire other Indigenous entrepreneurs, be role models for the girls and women in their community and close the gap between the earnings of Indigenous and non-Indigenous people.

"Indigenous people were the first entrepreneurs of Turtle Island," says Lynn-Marie. "Sisters Sage is actively healing and empowering our people through business."

GREAT IDEA!

Why Become an Entrepreneur?

Being an entrepreneur is about more than just making money. Entrepreneurs enjoy the pride—and risks—they take in working for themselves. They can set their own hours, and they become experts in money management, improve their communication skills and get to use their creativity.

As well, entrepreneurs get a buzz from seeing chances and opportunities where most people see problems. And great entrepreneurs know how to take advantage of those chances.

"Each product shares a unique story about our culture and traditions," says Lynn-Marie Angus (left), pictured here with her sister, Melissa-Rae.

BE FIERCE! BE STRONG!

Alex "Nemo" Hanse
(1988–)

GREAT IDEA!

Wearable Art

Madelyn Iler is a visual artist in Kingston, Ontario. She used to wipe excess paint off her canvases with old rags. Then she noticed how beautiful the rags were. She started using T-shirts to wipe off the paint.

Now Iler sells the colorful shirts as well as her paintings. People are delighted to wear her art or hang it on their walls.

Growing up poor meant Alex "Nemo" Hanse was picked on at school because of his old clothes. To earn some money, he started selling chips, candy and drinks.

At university Hanse became a rapper. He knew the importance of creating a brand to set him apart from other rappers. He and a friend talked about this but started feeling foolish, or foolie, as he called it, for spending so much time on it.

Then his friend asked, "What's a foolie?"

"I guess somebody who's dumb enough to try something," responded Hanse, "and figure it out in the end."

Hanse graduated from university in 2009 and kept rapping. He thought he could make extra money creating clothes for rappers, so he produced a T-shirt with *Foolies* on it. He posted photos of the shirt on Facebook and Twitter, and people wanted to buy it.

But Foolies clothes really started selling in 2015, when Hanse printed phrases on them such as *Be Fierce*

Like Taraji, Be Strong Like Regina or *Lead Like Ava*, which highlighted strong Black female actors Taraji P. Henson and Regina King, and filmmaker Ava DuVernay.

When *Essence*, a magazine for Black American women, asked Hanse for T-shirts for a Black Women in Hollywood event, the deadline was really tight. But Hanse knew the publicity would be incredible. He seized the opportunity and got the shirts there in time. The hard work paid off when sales of Foolies clothing and mugs soared.

Foolies hoodies, mugs, sweatshirts and T-shirts encourage people to overcome their fears.

"If you push through that feeling of being scared, that feeling of taking risk, really amazing things can happen."

—Marissa Mayer, former chief executive officer of Yahoo! Inc.

PASSWORD PROTECTED

Mira Modi

(2004–)

"It sounds a little crazy to buy a password," says Mira Modi. "But using a terrible password, such as *12345* or *password*, is even crazier." That belief led her to the idea of selling strong, secure passwords that are easy to remember.

Modi's business began when her mom asked her to generate some passwords. The 11-year-old New Yorker spotted an opportunity to start a business creating hard-to-hack passwords for other people. "Now we have such good computers, people can hack into anything so much more quickly," she says.

Modi uses Diceware to produce the passwords. It's a well-known system that has been used for decades. She rolls a die six times and writes down each number. Then she looks up that random six-digit number on a Diceware word list and matches the number to a word. Modi repeats her dice-throwing to generate six words that are easy for the customer to memorize but difficult for hackers to crack, since they're random.

SUCCESS!

THE SOUND OF BUSINESS

In 1996, when Daniel Ek was just 13 years old, he noticed that companies needed help with their websites. He decided to start a business designing and hosting sites for corporations. By the time he was 18, the Swedish computer whiz had a staff of 25.

But Ek also had a passion for music. So in 2006 he and his friend Martin Lorentzon created Spotify, the music-streaming service. Their timing was perfect—by age 35 Ek was a billionaire.

Modi writes out the words by hand and mails the list to her customer. "People are worried that I will take your passwords," she says, "but in reality I won't be able to remember them." She doesn't store them on her computer and recommends clients personalize their passwords by capitalizing letters or adding symbols.

School and homework mean that Modi can create passwords only at night and on weekends. But she's looking for ways to keep up with demand and expand her business.

It's vital that you use strong passwords on your devices. Mira Modi recognized this and created a business based on it.

"You have to make your own chances."
—Duncan Bannatyne, hotel and media entrepreneur

WARREN BUFFETT

Frederick Jones

WERNER 22

Lynda Kemp

CHAPTER THREE
DO WHAT YOU DO BEST

Successful entrepreneurs build on their strengths when starting a business.

That was the case with Victoria Alonsoperez from Uruguay. Even as a young student, she excelled at science and engineering.

When she was older, she studied electrical and space engineering in university. One day, while working as a teaching associate for the International Space University in France, she decided to enter a competition. Remembering the **foot-and-mouth disease** that had destroyed much of the cattle industry in Uruguay in 2001, she used her engineering skills to create a product that could track livestock and detect health problems early. She not only won the contest but was also awarded funding to start a business. Alonsoperez had never considered becoming an entrepreneur, but winning the competition created an accidental opportunity, and she took it. Soon Chipsafer was born, a company that produces solar-powered collars that track cattle remotely to monitor their health. Despite the challenges of establishing a new business, Alonsoperez believes she's learned to make "the best of every opportunity."

"Do not focus on numbers. Focus on doing what you do best. It's about building community who want to visit your site every day because you create value and offer expertise."

—Cassey Ho, founder of Blogilates.com

Like Alonsoperez, Brad Ludden used his expertise to help others. When Ludden's aunt developed breast cancer, Ludden wanted to help. He decided to use his skills as a competitive kayaker to create First Descents, a company providing free outdoor adventures for cancer patients between the ages of 18 and 39. As Ludden continued to excel in his sport, he found more sponsors for First Descents. In 2020 he established Hero Recharge, a program to help COVID-19 health workers deal with the stress of their work.

THE NUMBERS GUY

Warren Buffett

(1930–)

As a kid, Warren Buffett could calculate complex columns of numbers in his head. He was six when he decided to use his skill to start his first business—buying and selling bottles of Coke. At 11 he dove into the roller-coaster world of finance and learned valuable lessons about patience when he sold his stock too early. As a teenager he washed cars, delivered newspapers and bought **pinball machines** to install in local businesses.

Buffett completed college in three years, then continued his studies at Columbia University with Ben Graham, a brilliant investor who would become his mentor. Buffett was so keen to learn that he was the only student to earn an A+ in Graham's finance class. After graduating, Buffett began investing and teaching night classes at the University of Omaha. When his mentor offered him a job as a stockbroker, Buffett jumped at the opportunity, and he and his wife moved to New York.

As Buffett learned more about finances, he developed his own theories about business. He believed the key to a good company was how well it was managed and run. As he followed his business beliefs, Buffett's wealth grew. Yet, despite making lots of money, he didn't live a fancy lifestyle.

In 2006 Buffett announced that he planned to donate more than 80 percent of his money to charitable causes. Much of that would go to the Bill and Melinda Gates Foundation, which focuses on world health and education issues (see chapter 10). Buffett and Gates, the founder of tech giant Microsoft, had become close friends and believed in the same goal of making the world a better place.

"If you get to my age in life and nobody thinks well of you, I don't care how big your bank account is, your life is a disaster."

—Warren Buffett, businessman and philanthropist

Warren Buffett visits the stock exchange to watch financial deals take place in person.

FREDERICK COULD FIX ANYTHING

Frederick Jones

(1893–1961)

Frederick Jones loved to take things apart and put them back together.

Abandoned by his mother soon after his birth, Jones was raised by his father until he was seven. When his poverty-stricken father could no longer care for his son, he placed him in the care of the Catholic Church.

There Jones's skill at mechanics was appreciated. Despite that, he ran off at age 11 to Cincinnati, where he found a job in a garage. By the time he was 14, he was supervising work in the garage.

For the next 20 years, Jones worked in the South and the Midwest of the United States. Despite his mechanical expertise, he had trouble finding jobs. Jones was bi-racial and, because of that, faced **discrimination**. But he persisted and landed a variety of jobs, repairing cars, furnaces, farm equipment and steamships.

In 1913, while working as a janitor and repairman in a Minneapolis hotel, a guest recognized his mechanical

> "If someday they say of me that in my work I have contributed something to the welfare and happiness of my fellow man, I shall be satisfied."
>
> —George Westinghouse, entrepreneur

Frederick Jones checks out equipment. He wanted everything he invented to work well.

ability and offered him a job on his farm in Hallock, Minnesota. Jones was happy in Hallock, repairing machinery and cars on the farm. He also became involved in the community, pursued his love of car racing and took a correspondence course in electrical engineering. He said he'd finally found a place where you were judged for your character and ability, not the color of your skin.

Jones joined the army in World War I. Soon his superiors realized how good Jones was at fixing machinery, and his work was in great demand. When the war ended, Jones returned to Hallock and began inventing. One of his first inventions was a soundtrack unit for motion pictures.

Entrepreneur Joseph A. Numero was impressed and hired Jones. Soon Jones secured his first **patent**—a movie-ticket machine. More inventions followed, including a refrigerated unit for trucks to transport food. Numero and Jones established the US Thermo Control Company (later Thermo King Corporation). Not only did their company thrive, but the refrigerated unit Jones invented became essential in World War II to transport blood.

SUCCESS!

MAKING THINGS GO

Inventor, engineer and entrepreneur George Westinghouse started his first company at age 23. He held more than 300 patents and started 60 companies. Westinghouse's work helped railroads grow by promoting the use of electricity in transportation.

DRESS-UP IS FUN

Lynda Kemp
(1953–2016)

SUCCESS!

FOR THE LOVE OF BOOKS AND MUSIC

Judy and Hy Sarick combined their business skills and passion for kids' books and music to establish the Children's Book Store in Toronto in 1974. The store grew to become one of the largest children's bookstores in the world, drawing writers, illustrators, librarians, teachers and readers of all ages.

Lynda Kemp loved making her own costumes and dressing up. She loved dressing up her little brother too.

Kemp learned how to sew and knit from her grandma Rose, an expert seamstress in Toronto's fur industry. But by the time Kemp entered university, she had decided to follow another passion—acting.

Kemp soon combined her love of sewing and acting by working as a wardrobe designer for movies and acting in shows like *Polka Dot Door*, a Canadian children's program.

She also began buying costumes from producers after shows were over—sometimes for as little as a dollar. When Kemp's garage was packed with costumes, her brother asked her what she was going to do with all of them. "I'm going to make a costume company," she replied. And she did. She named her company Thunder Thighs, Kemp's nickname as an actor.

In the mid-1980s Kemp and her husband moved their growing company to a sprawling old warehouse in downtown Toronto. Thunder Thighs Costumes soon attracted customers from the busy film and television industry in Toronto, such as famous actors Diane Keaton and Alan Rickman, who played Professor Snape in the Harry Potter movies. They knew Kemp's passion for sewing and admired her vast knowledge, especially about clothing from other eras.

As her business grew, Kemp continued to buy costumes from films, auctions and antique shops. She sewed many costumes herself and adapted others. She even altered an antique wedding dress for her sister-in-law, and after the wedding she rented the dress out for film and television brides.

Kemp's business became one of the most successful costume stores in Canada, and it continues to thrive.

GREAT IDEA!

Emma Knows Tomatoes

Emma Biggs loved to work alongside her dad in the garden. She especially loved growing tomatoes. By the time she was a teen, that passion had grown into a successful career as a garden writer, blogger, speaker and entrepreneur selling tomato seeds from her home and garden in Toronto.

Lynda Kemp had fun giving her dressed-up son a ride when he was younger.

CHAPTER FOUR

YOU'RE NEVER TOO OLD... OR TOO YOUNG

Streetcar conductor, railroad worker, lawyer—Harland Sanders tried all these jobs but couldn't stick to any of them. It wasn't until 1952, when he was 62 years old, that Sanders shared his secret fried-chicken recipe with a Utah restaurant owner, and his career took off.

Soon other restaurant owners wanted to buy a **franchise**, or pay for the right to sell Sanders's chicken. Kentucky Fried Chicken (KFC) was a hit. By the time Sanders died in 1980, there were more than 6,000 KFC restaurants in 48 countries around the world.

Maya Penn, from Atlanta, Georgia, learned how to **code** and animate her own stories when she was just four years old. Four years later she went in a different direction, starting an eco-friendly fashion company called Maya's Ideas. She sells everything from scarves and hats to bags and jewelry. The items are made from organic cotton and bamboo and are colored using fruit and vegetable dyes instead of harmful chemicals.

> "If you begin, you win."
> —Richie Norton, digital entrepreneur

In 2011, when Penn was 11, she founded Maya's Ideas 4 The Planet. This nonprofit organization fights for environmental change and also encourages girls to get involved in tech careers.

Young or old—entrepreneurs can be any age. Some have been overlooked because people have assumed they're too old to work, while others are ignored because they're kids. But kidpreneurs or seniorpreneurs can overcome any obstacle if they believe in their idea.

H3Y! APP

Chen Yuheng

(2004–)

GREAT IDEA!

Business Fairs for Kids

Acton Children's Business Fairs have taken place in more than 200 cities around the world to showcase companies created and launched by kids. Children sell products, everything from candy and sushi to jewelry, and services, such as performing card tricks or taking photos. Over 30,000 kids have taken part, selling their products and learning about running a business. Look online to see if there's one coming to your area and find out if you can get involved.

Chen Yuheng was only 11 years old when he began creating his own social media **app**. He realized that the most popular social media apps in China, where he lived, were developed for the older generation. The content didn't interest young people, and the apps provided little privacy.

An app aimed at teenagers could be very successful, Chen figured. He didn't let his age stop him from getting to work on his idea. In fact, he recruited his brother, Chen Yurong, who's two years younger, to help him build it.

At first the app was named Hey to reflect the enthusiastic way teenagers approach new things. Then, to make the app's name a little different, Chen replaced the *e* of Hey with a 3.

H3Y! launched in December 2015. It features information about movies and celebrities, as well as cute backgrounds, green-screen live video chats and off-the-wall functions. The app includes gesture-based navigation that saves time, as well as a customizable interface. No wonder that in just one month more than 21,000 users registered for H3Y!

By the time Chen was 13, he was one of the world's youngest self-made millionaires. The Chen brothers were soon leading a team of about 20 employees. If most kids owned such a successful company, they'd quit school. Not Chen. "Even Bill Gates finished primary and secondary school," he says. (See more about Bill Gates on page 78.)

(See more about Bill Gates on page 78.)

"Do not despise little beginnings."

—Andrena Sawyer, president of P.E.R.K. (Passion. Experience. Relevance. Knowledge.) Consulting

Recognizing what teens like and how they use social media made Chen Yuheng's H3Y! app a success.

SWEET REWARDS

Harbhajan Kaur

(1925–)

SUCCESS!

ENTREPRENEUR STUDENTS

Students in the fourth and fifth grades at Pelmo Park Public School in Toronto are already learning entrepreneurial skills. One group has marketed slime as a tool to reduce fidgeting and stress, while another wrote proposals for T-shirts promoting the Black Lives Matter movement.

The entrepreneur program helps the kids learn new math and technology concepts. As well, it introduces students from **marginalized** groups to the idea of building businesses in their communities.

When Harbhajan Kaur of Chandigarh, India, was 90, she realized she had one regret about her long life: she'd never earned any money on her own. This quiet stay-at-home mom made up her mind that it wasn't too late to change that. She is a great cook, so she decided to sell besan barfi, a creamy treat consisting of besan (flour made from ground yellow lentils), condensed milk and sugar, at a local organic market.

Although Kaur was shy, she was soon chatting happily with customers as she sold her sweets. On her first day she made 2,000 rupees (about 27 US dollars or 35 Canadian). Kaur's earnings not only made her proud but also gave her the confidence to develop her business. Soon she was also making delicious chutneys, marmalades and pickles.

Kaur's granddaughter helped by branding and creating packaging for Kaur's products. To remind customers of their own grandmothers, the Kaurs chose the slogan

Bachpan yaad aajayegi, which means "You'll remember your childhood."

When Anand Mahindra, an Indian businessman and billionaire, heard about Kaur's story, he was quick to post a tweet about it, calling her his entrepreneur of the year. Her phone is constantly ringing, with people wanting to order her products. Kaur is careful to pace herself so she doesn't become overworked doing the cooking she so enjoys.

"Life is all about evolving," says Kaur. "You will do new things only when you learn new things."

"Define success in your own terms, achieve it by your own rules, and build a life you're proud to live."

—Anne Sweeney, former co-chair of Disney Media Networks

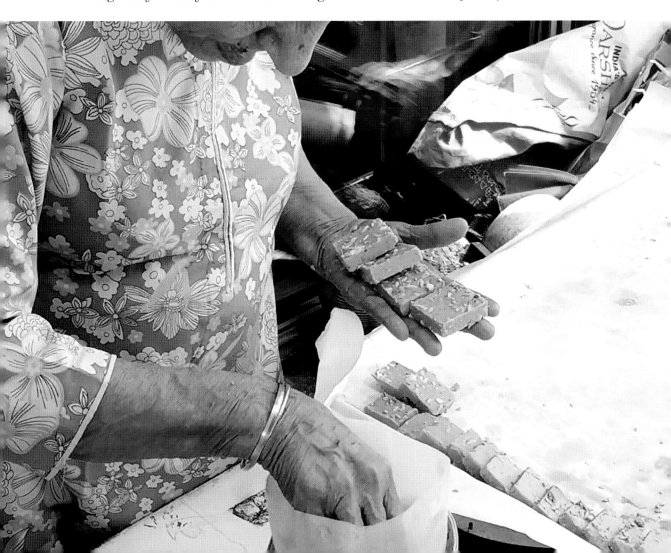

Harbhajan Kaur's besan barfi is delicious and changed her life when she was in her 90s.

MO'S BOWS

Moziah Bridges
(2001–)

"I started my company because I needed an accessory to help me look sharp," says Moziah Bridges of Memphis, "but didn't see anything out there that fit my style or personality." Bridges was only nine years old when he started making his own bow ties. Soon he was selling them to other kids at school after they saw how great he looked.

Bridges now creates bow ties, neckties and pocket squares. Mo's Bows are sold online, as well as in stores across the United States. During the COVID-19 **pandemic**, Bridges pivoted to sell face masks also. To help other entrepreneurs improve their businesses, he advises them to work on what he calls the four *p*'s: place, price, promotion and product.

When you're a kidpreneur, it can be tough to be taken seriously. Bridges encourages other young businesspeople to smile, speak up, care about their appearance, have a firm handshake and be passionate about their product. "Don't worry about the competition," he says. "Instead, *become* the competition by anticipating the newest trends."

GREAT IDEA!

Artistic Accessories

Fun, funky and functional is how Madelyn Rich describes the accessories available on her website, Accents by Madelyn. She first sold her hand-knitted gloves and neck warmers as a side business while working as a paralegal and social worker. After retiring, she really developed her business.

Some people think seniorpreneurs are too old to use social media, e-commerce and online **analytics**. But Rich recognizes their importance. And during the COVID-19 pandemic, she was able to revamp and offer specially fitted 3-D masks.

For Bridges, the word *bows* is an abbreviation for *believe* in yourself, find *opportunities* to give back, *work* hard and *seek* support from friends and family. Bridges helps out his community through the Go Mo! Summer Camp Scholarship Fund and the Mo's Bows Foundation, which builds youth and family leadership through entrepreneurship.

Moziah Bridges has incredible style—and business sense.

"Figure out what you like doing, then find out how you can make money doing it, then just let your passion drive your business."

—Moziah Bridges,
chief executive officer
of Mo's Bows

STEVEN SPIELBERG

ASIA NEWSON

THE NEW YORK PUBLIC

MARTIN RADTKE

CHAPTER FIVE

TAKE ADVICE FROM PEOPLE YOU ADMIRE

Smart entrepreneurs listen to the advice of other wise and experienced business owners. They learn how to benefit from their failures and success.

Samantha John and Jocelyn Leavitt **collaborated** to create the Hopscotch app, which teaches kids computer programming. John's background as a **programmer**, **software developer** and engineer, coupled with Leavitt's experience as a teacher, helped them set up their new business, as did the advice of Alan Kay, one of the pioneers of programming and computer science. John and Leavitt also paid attention to their team's suggestions about running the company. "It's very important to me to listen to people I'm working with," says John.

Learning from experts, listening to co-workers and using personal experiences also helped computer engineer Rainier Mallol, from the Dominican Republic.

When Mallol was 14, his mom came down with a terrible disease called **dengue fever**. Mallol wanted to help, but what could a kid do? When he was older, he found a way. He became involved in a program at **NASA (the National Aeronautics and Space Administration)** that used information to predict where disease outbreaks would occur. That meant doctors could take steps to stop the spread of a disease like dengue fever before it killed many people.

Soon Mallol teamed up with public health specialist Dr. Dhesi Raja to develop AIME, a program that uses artificial intelligence to predict dengue fever outbreaks. Mallol knew that sharing information would help people take action before an outbreak occurred. "Dengue fever is just the start," says Mallol. "We will create a device to diagnose tuberculosis and malaria."

By working with other experts to create a useful medical tool, Mallol not only helped save lives but also created a successful business. It's clear after the outbreak of COVID-19 in 2020 that tools like AIME will become increasingly important as the world prepares to deal with future diseases.

ALL LIT UP

Asia Newson

(2003–)

When Asia Newson was five, she wanted to start a business like her dad's. He sold candles, and she wanted to do that too. She felt that being her own boss would also give her freedom. Her mom had a regular job and had to get up early and work hard all day for someone else. She would come home tired, and Newson didn't see her as much as she wanted to. Newson thought that being an entrepreneur gave a person freedom to make up their own hours.

But how do you start a business when you're just a kid?

First Newson learned to make her own candles. She sold them in downtown Detroit and door-to-door, under her dad's supervision. When she was little, Newson noted, people bought candles because they thought she was "cute," but as she got older, security guards started kicking her off their property.

How could she continue to sell? Her mother suggested she get a business license, and Newson followed her advice. After that, when she was stopped she pulled out her license and said, "Here, you see?" She also found support from local businesspeople in Detroit, who admired her business savvy, sparkling personality and determination.

GREAT IDEA!

A Passion to Help

Rich Horgan's younger brother has Duchenne muscular dystrophy, a rare and deadly disease. His brother's illness propelled Horgan to start a nonprofit **biotechnology** company, Cure Rare Disease. Horgan studied at Harvard Business School and collaborated with experts, not only to make his business a success but also to help researchers find or create medicines to help those with rare diseases get better.

Newson used their help to improve her product and packaging. She also created a company with her mom, called Super Business Girl, and taught other kids how to become entrepreneurs. She appreciates the advice she received and wants to pass on her knowledge to other kids who want to become entrepreneurs. She believes that sharing her knowledge of business is important.

"With the candles that they make, we go outside, and I assign kids to their mentors and we start selling candles. Once it's over, we come back to my office and we talk about the experience, what we learned and what we could have done better."

—Asia Newson, entrepreneur

Young business-minded girls, including Asia Newson, get together to talk about ideas and plans.

FOR THE LOVE OF MOVIES

Steven Spielberg
(1946–)

Steven Spielberg was always fascinated by movies, and he started making his own when he was a child. By the time he was 12, he had filmed a movie from a script and used real actors. As a teen, he charged 25 cents admission to watch his home movies while his sister sold popcorn. When he was 17 he filmed *Firelight,* a feature-length science-fiction movie.

Spielberg also watched every movie he could. When he moved to California as a young man, he talked his way onto movie sets to watch films being made, and he worked as an **intern**. Spielberg learned how to make good movies by analyzing them and speaking to directors and producers whose work he admired. In 1969 his short film *Amblin'* won awards at film festivals.

Spielberg continued to make films on a wide variety of subjects—sharks in *Jaws,* aliens in *E.T. the Extra-Terrestrial,* science fiction in *Close Encounters of the Third Kind* and dinosaurs in *Jurassic Park.* He collaborated with other directors, writers and producers, including George Lucas of *Star Wars.* Spielberg created

> **"An essential aspect of creativity is not being afraid to fail."**
>
> —Edward Land,
> scientist and inventor

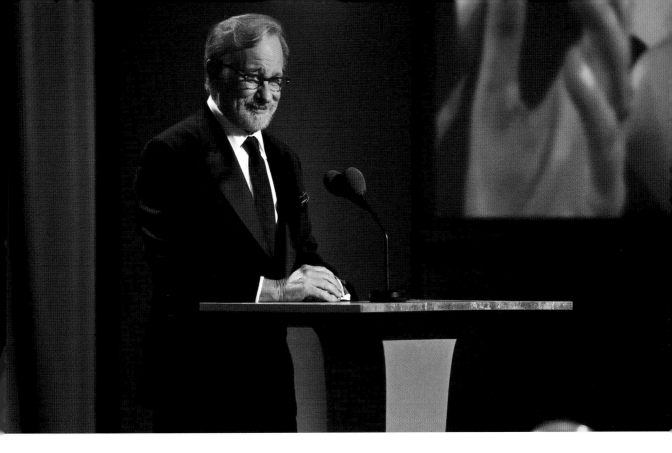

Steven Spielberg honors his fellow artists at an awards ceremony.

the movie studio DreamWorks with partners Jeffrey Katzenberg and David Geffen. Many of his movies were financially successful, but not all. "I'm not really interested in making money," says Spielberg. "That comes as a result of success." However, he never stopped innovating and following his passion for telling important stories, such as *Schindler's List*.

Schindler's List was based on the true story of a Polish man who risked his life to save 1,100 Jews from death in Nazi **concentration camps**. The movie earned Spielberg praise and awards. He used profits from the film to set up the USC Shoah Foundation, a nonprofit group that has preserved the testimonies of people who lived through horrific experiences during the Holocaust, when six million Jews were killed by the Nazis.

SUCCESS!

MOVIEMAKERS

Some actors also become movie producers. They use their knowledge of acting and suggestions from directors and producers they respect to produce movies of their own. A few famous actors who are also movie producers are Natalie Portman, George Clooney and Drew Barrymore.

Inscribed here are the words of an
immigrant whose life was transformed by the
Library and whose estate now enriches it.

IN MEMORY

MARTIN RADTKI

1883–1973

I had little opportunity for formal education
as a young man in Lithuania, and I am deeply
indebted to The New York Public Library
for the opportunity to educate myself.
In appreciation, I have given the Library
my estate with the wish that it be used so
that others can have the same opportunity
made available to me.

THE LIBRARY WAS HIS TEACHER

Martin Radtke
(1883–1973)

"Life is too short to learn from your own mistakes, so learn from other people's mistakes."

—Geoffrey Woo, co-founder and chief executive officer of HVMN (formerly Nootrobox)

When Martin Radtke died, few people knew him. He was a quiet man who'd emigrated from Lithuania in 1913, when he was 30. Although poor and unable to read when he arrived in New York City, he soon made a decision that changed his life. He began going to the library, where he not only learned to read but also studied economics from books he read there.

Radtke used what he'd learned from books and magazines written by experts in economics to buy **stocks** in the 1930s. He never sold the stocks and gradually amassed a fortune. "He held on to what he had and watched it grow," says his Wall Street broker, George A. Garjian. He also says that Radtke went to the library three times a week to read and study until the day he died. Garjian joked that Radtke "was in the library so often you might as well give them money."

Little did he know that was exactly what Radtke would do. When Radtke died he willed $368,000 to the library.

The library was so awed by his gift, especially at a time when it was in desperate need of funds, that the folks there decided to do something unusual. They installed a plaque to Radtke at the entrance to the main branch of the New York City Library at 42nd Street and Fifth Avenue.

Today if you walk up the stairs, past the stone lions and into the magnificent main building of the library, you can read Radtke's words:

I had little opportunity for formal education as a young man in Lithuania, and I am deeply indebted to the New York Public Library for the opportunity to educate myself. In appreciation, I have given the library my estate with the wish that others can have the same opportunity made available to me.

GREAT IDEA!

He Built Libraries

After making a fortune in steel, Andrew Carnegie was one of the richest men in the world. Then he did something amazing. In the early 1900s he began to give his fortune away to fund public libraries around the world. Carnegie never forgot how libraries had helped him acquire knowledge. When he was 17 and a Scottish immigrant to the United States, he'd written a letter to a Pittsburgh newspaper in which he complained that the local library didn't allow everyone access to books, plus it charged a fee he couldn't afford. As a result of his letter, that library changed its policy.

The magnificent 42nd Street library in New York City welcomes readers.

CHAPTER SIX

BE A PLANNER

Even very young entrepreneurs recognize the need for planning and thinking ahead.

Sofia Overton started her company, Wise Pocket Products, at age 11 after seeing her cousin stick her phone in her boot because she had no pockets. Overton wanted to give active kids like her cousin an easily accessible place to keep their phones, so she came up with the idea of making socks with pockets.

Overton went on the TV show *Shark Tank*. Her presentation impressed the show's investors, and she received funding for her new product.

Overton decided that for every pair of socks sold, she'd donate a pair to a child in need. "Wise Pocket Products believes that if you make sure a child has warm feet, they will always have a warm heart knowing that their community cares for them," she says. Overton has also expanded her business to include leggings with pockets.

Like Overton, Shivani Siroya knows that thinking ahead while being flexible to changing circumstances is important for creating a good business. Siroya studied economics, worked in economic-development programs and interviewed 3,500 people before she decided to launch her company Tala in 2011. Tala loans money to small businesses in developing countries such as Kenya, Mexico, India, the Philippines and Tanzania. Siroya believes that knowing her clients personally builds trust. "I realized that I trusted Seema because I had gotten to know her," she says about a woman running a small jewelry business in India. "And she paid me back because she trusted me too and knew that I would be there for her again if she needed me."

Siroya's company created an app that is easy to use and gives clients round-the-clock access to customer service. The result? Loyal clients who spread the word about Tala.

> "Someone is sitting in the shade today because someone planted a tree long ago."
>
> —Warren Buffett, financier

PAYING ATTENTION

Ted Turner
(1938–)

Ted Turner was always a risk taker and a planner. He worked hard, paid attention to changing tastes and trends and was ready to try something new. He spoke his mind, even when he was criticized for his strong opinions.

Turner was plunged into the business world when his father died suddenly in 1963, leaving 24-year-old Ted to take over his advertising company. Turner paid off his father's debts and made the business successful again. Once he'd set that business on a solid course, Turner looked for new opportunities while pursuing his love of sports, especially sailing.

In 1979 Turner entered his new sailboat in a race from Plymouth, England, to Fastnet Rock, off the coast of Ireland. A terrible storm hit, and many boats capsized— 22 people drowned. Despite the terrifying and dangerous conditions, Turner never turned his boat back. He kept on sailing and won the race.

In 1980 Turner launched CNN, a nonstop news channel. Many people said it would never succeed. But they were wrong. CNN became hugely successful. After

GREAT IDEA!

Newspapers Can Make a Positive Difference

After her husband Philip's death in 1963, Katherine Graham took over as head of the *Washington Post* newspaper. It was rare in those days for a woman to run a newspaper, but Katharine believed in her paper and in her reporters' ability to uncover the truth and tell a story well. Two of her reporters, Carl Bernstein and Bob Woodward, played a major role in uncovering the illegal actions of the US president, Richard Nixon, which led to his resignation in August 1974.

creating CNN, Turner looked for new business ventures. In 1986 he bought a large film library, including classics like *Casablanca* and *Gone with the Wind*. Many people wondered why he'd bought so many old movies, but he considered it a good idea and a smart deal, and he was right. People like watching old movies.

Over the years Turner has not only made billions creating new companies and pursuing innovative ideas, but he has also financially supported environmental causes, solar energy, the United Nations and **nuclear disarmament**.

Ted Turner enjoys sharing his ideas and opinions on TV.

SOUNDS GOOD!

Amar Bose
(1929–2013)

"Always deliver more than expected."

—Larry Page,
co-founder of Google

As a kid, Amar Bose spent hours taking radios apart and putting them back together. By the time he was 11, he was using his skill in electronics to repair radios and help supplement his family's income. His parents were so impressed with his talent that they encouraged him to apply to the Massachusetts Institute of Technology (MIT), one of the best science-focused universities in the world. And that's where Bose went to study in 1947.

Not only did he complete his bachelor of science at MIT, but he also obtained a doctorate in electrical engineering and worked there as a professor. He enjoyed teaching students how to solve problems.

One day in his early years as a teacher, Bose bought a stereo system so he could listen to music. Although he'd purchased what he thought were good speakers, he was disappointed. He didn't like the sound they produced. He was sure he could design better ones. After all, he'd studied acoustics, the science of sound. All he needed was funding to design the speakers and start a business.

Bose approached investors with his ideas, and they agreed to give him the money he needed. Soon Bose patented his new speakers and founded a company that focused on building sound systems.

Bose's company was successful—people who bought his speakers said they felt like they were enjoying music in a concert hall. Although his company made him wealthy, he said, "I never went into business to make money. I went into business so that I could do interesting things that hadn't been done before."

"What do you need to start a business? Three simple things: know your product better than anyone, know your customer, and have a burning desire to succeed."

—Dave Thomas, founder of Wendy's

Amar Bose was proud of his successful company and sound products.

INSPIRED BY THE WORLD

Dame Anita Roddick
(1942–2007)

Anita Perella loved to travel. After finishing school, she worked in Paris and Geneva, then traveled through Europe, the South Pacific and Africa. As she explored new countries, she learned about natural products people around the world used to stay healthy.

When Perella came home to England, she married Gordon Roddick. They opened a bed-and-breakfast and a restaurant. But after a few years, Roddick's husband wanted to fulfill his dream of riding a horse from Buenos Aires to New York. The only problem for Anita was how to support herself and their two daughters while her husband was away. Her solution was to open a store that would sell back-to-nature cosmetics inspired by her travels.

Roddick didn't have a lot of money, so she knew she had to be creative with her new business. She painted her store green to hide old spots on the walls. She used interviews to spread news about her innovative products and her business inspiration. She hired good staff.

SUCCESS!

SAFE FOR BABY

Jessica Alba is a busy, successful actor. After her first child was born, Alba was worried that her baby could have allergic reactions to some of the baby products on the market, just as she had when she was a kid. Alba decided to launch the Honest Company to make baby products free of harmful chemicals. Her company has been hugely successful.

The Body Shop's natural products are sold all over the world.

"The original Body Shop was a series of brilliant accidents," Roddick said. "It had a great smell, it had a funky name...We knew about storytelling then, so all our products had stories. We recycled everything, not because we were environmentally friendly, but because we didn't have enough bottles. It was a good idea."

The combination of natural products, support for the environment and passionate staff made the store a success. Soon many Body Shops were opened in Europe and the United States.

When Dame Anita died in 2007, she left her fortune to charities she believed would help make local communities and the world a better place.

Sissi Chao

JEAN BOSCO NZEYIMANA

Alex Schulze

Andrew Cooper

4ocean

CHAPTER SEVEN
GO GREEN

When Ingvar Kamprad was just five years old, he decided he wanted to earn some money for his family. He began selling matches to neighbors. Twelve years later he set up his own company, called IKEA—his initials, plus *E* for Elmtaryd (his family farm's name) and *A* for Agunnaryd (a nearby village).

In 1948 Kamprad started selling furniture, and since 2008 IKEA has been the world's largest furniture seller. Its environmental action plan focuses on reducing energy use and harmful chemicals, sourcing wood from responsibly managed forests, using only recyclable materials for flat packaging and more. IKEA also works with UNICEF and Save the Children to help kids around the world.

GREAT IDEA!

Ditch the Bottles

Ben Stern of Melbourne, Florida, was troubled by the number of plastic bottles that end up in the trash. That inspired him to start making Nohbo personal-care products in 2014, when he was just 14. Nohbo stands for "NO Hair BOttles."

Nohbo drops are water-soluble pods that contain soap for your hair or body. The drops don't come in bottles and contain no harsh chemicals, which makes them very eco-friendly. They're one of the world's first single-use and eco-friendly personal-care products.

Many entrepreneurs find success when they put caring for the environment at the top of their list of goals. Recycling, making environmentally friendly products and cleaning up garbage are all ways these ecopreneurs create prosperous companies.

Green Toys Inc. was founded in 2007 by Laurie Hyman and Robert von Goeben, thanks to Laurie's determination to find better toys for her family. The company makes environmentally responsible toys using recycled plastic and other eco-friendly materials. So far the company has recycled more than 104 million milk jugs to make toys that range from arts and crafts sets and fire trucks to submarines and skipping ropes.

Green Toys' founders believe that the best way to encourage environmental change is through items people use every day. Even the packaging for their products is eco-friendly, made of 100 percent recycled cardboard.

HELP YOUR COMMUNITY

Jean Bosco Nzeyimana
(1993–)

SUCCESS!

GREEN PICKUP

While working at a recording studio in Vancouver, British Columbia, Lisa von Sturmer was amazed by how much organic waste her workplace created. She started a service to pick up this waste, as well as recyclables.

Soon von Sturmer's company, Growing City, had seven trucks making pickups. Thanks to her service, companies can reduce their waste by more than half. "Don't hold on to mistakes," she advises other entrepreneurs. "Learn from them, never repeat them."

When Jean Bosco Nzeyimana was a child growing up in Nyamagabe, Rwanda, he was very poor. His tiny village had no electricity or roads and little clean water. The community burned wood for cooking. To get that wood, the villagers cut down trees, which caused soil **erosion**. Nzeyimana also noticed that there were many landfills, or garbage dumps, around his village.

When he was 19, Nzeyimana came up with a solution to both the **deforestation** and landfill problems. He decided to turn **organic waste**, such as food scraps, into energy. To do this he created a machine that compresses the waste into briquettes (small blocks) and pellets for cooking. "This enabled our communities not only to have clean fuel alternatives to wood charcoal," Nzeyimana says, "but also to increase sanitation in communities."

This "wastepreneur" founded a company called Habona, which means "illumination," and also began making fertilizer for farmers. At first Nzeyimana had to train workers himself, since most had never even seen briquettes before. But he worked hard, and the company's customers soon included restaurants, schools and government offices. Nzeyimana has won many prizes for his work, including being named Top Young Entrepreneur of Rwanda.

With plans to expand the company to other parts of Africa, Nzeyimana hopes to create jobs to give more people a chance to earn money and support their families. He also volunteers in his community's Cooperative for Environment and **Biodiversity** Conservation.

"Never start a business just to 'make money.' Start a business to make a difference."

—Marie Forleo, host of *MarieTV*

At the 2016 Global Entrepreneurship Summit, Jean Bosco Nzeyimana (middle) was part of a panel discussion led by then US president Barack Obama (left). Other panel members included (left to right) entrepreneurs Mai Medhat and Mariana Costa Checa, and Meta CEO Mark Zuckerberg.

ENVIRONMENTAL FASHION

Sissi Chao
(1989–)

Sissi Chao started her recycling company because of a dream in which she held the planet in her hands.

Sissi Chao's parents were horrified when she started REMAKEHUB in 2018. She'd studied business in the United Kingdom and in the United States and should have a great job, her parents felt. Instead she'd chosen to work with trash!

Why? When Chao returned to her home in China after her studies, she started working in her parents' clothing factory. But she was shocked by how much pollution the business created. "I decided to tell my parents that I would not continue to work on the pollution side," says Chao, "but on the solution side."

Chao uses technology and creative design to deal with the waste. She recycles it and turns it into a **renewable resource** so future generations will have less pollution to deal with. REMAKEHUB's projects have included using coffee grounds to make mugs, recycling plastic bottles into clothing and making buttons and zippers from thrown-away fruit and clothing waste. "There is no way that we cannot move

towards sustainability," says Chao. "It's the only choice left." The company is also working to take fishing nets that have been dumped into the ocean and recycle them into sunglasses and office chairs.

Starting REMAKEHUB has changed the way Chao shops. She buys fewer clothes and recycles them when she's finished with them. And now her parents are very proud of their daughter and her title—the "Princess of Waste."

"We need people to do better for our planet," says Sissi Chao. "We need businesses to do better as well."

SUCCESS!

SHOP PACKAGE-FREE

The Tare Shop in Halifax sells everything from makeup and reusable food wrap to bulk foods such as chickpeas and chocolate chips. But what's different about this store is that it provides package-free shopping.

Kate Pepler opened the store in 2018 after feeling overwhelmed by the amount of pollution in the world. About one-third of the waste Canadian families generate is food packaging. Pepler encourages customers to bring their own containers to her store and donates a portion of its profits to groups suggested by customers.

AN OCEAN OF OPPORTUNITY

Andrew Cooper
(1990–)

and Alex Schulze
(1991–)

GREAT IDEA!

Dressing for Green Success

Beulah is a British clothing company started in 2010 by Lady Natasha Rufus Isaacs and Lavinia Brennan to provide jobs for women. In India, women who are disadvantaged or were in the sex trade print and sew fabric for the company. Women in Nepal weave wool and silk for Beulah, and their earnings support their community. Now the firm's clothes are worn by many famous women, including the Duchess of Cambridge.

Beulah works hard to minimize its environmental impact. The company focuses on using natural fibers, which biodegrade more quickly than artificial fabrics. Beulah also invests 10 percent of its profits into projects that support vulnerable women and provides employment for them.

A year after Andrew Cooper and Alex Schulze finished their college business degrees in 2014, they headed to Bali to go surfing. But when they got there, they were shocked at how much trash was on the beach. A lifeguard told them the beach was cleaned every morning, but more garbage washed in throughout the day. The friends were upset—and jolted into starting a business.

Cooper and Schulze formed the company 4ocean to remove plastic and glass waste from oceans and coastlines around the world. The entrepreneurs from Florida turn that trash into bracelets and iPhone cases that they sell to pay for collecting more trash. The duo also raises money selling such items as reusable bottles and environmentally friendly T-shirts.

Since 2017 the company has removed more than 21 million pounds (9.5 million kilograms) of trash from the ocean. As well as pulling out trash with nets, 4ocean crews drive specially designed **mobile** skimmers that grab the garbage. They also use floating barriers known as boom systems to stop plastic from reaching the ocean.

Only 9 percent of all plastic ever made has been recycled, but Cooper and Schulze aim to improve on that. "This is our opportunity to clean the ocean and change the course of history for generations to come," says Schulze. "Together, we can end the ocean plastic crisis."

"The most sustainable way is to not make things. The second most sustainable way is to make something very useful, to solve a problem that hasn't been solved."

—Thomas Sigsgaard, architect

4Ocean cleanup crews have pulled more than 21 million pounds (9.5 million kilograms) of trash from the waters around Bali and Java.

DIVYANK TURAKHIA

LONNIE JOHNSON

SEO

Oprah Winfrey

CHAPTER EIGHT

FIND YOUR NICHE

Anneke van den Broek, an animal lover since she was a child, was having trouble finding natural, high-quality products for her pets. So in 2008 this Australian entrepreneur gave up a career in business and marketing to start Rufus & Coco. The pet-care company has now expanded to nine countries and sells everything from natural kitty litter and grooming brushes to dog collars and toys.

Discovering what really interests you is an important part of being an entrepreneur. It allows these business-people to not only enjoy their work but also to find the tenacity to continue when times are tough.

> "Entrepreneurs have a mindset that sees the possibilities rather than the problems created by change."
>
> —J. Gregory Dees, founder and director of the Center for Social Entrepreneurship Development

Chen Yue-Chia was born in Taiwan and came to the United States when she was three. She later changed her name to Sue Chen. After she graduated from university, her uncles in Taiwan, who made mobility products such as canes and walkers, asked her to look over a contract they were considering with an American company. When Chen advised them not to sign the deal, her uncles became angry and made her feel foolish.

But Chen realized she had a real interest in mobility products. When her grandfather suggested she start her own company for the products, she decided to follow his advice. Chen founded NOVA Medical Products in 1993. By listening to her customers' suggestions, she created an award-winning company. She also donates walkers, wheelchairs and more to people in developing countries.

TEEN TECH SUCCESS

Divyank Turakhia

(1982–)

SUCCESS!

BLENDING CULTURES

Chieko Aoki's career in hotel management began accidentally when her husband's construction company became a partner in a hotel chain in Brazil. The more the Japanese-born businesswoman worked in hotel management, the more she enjoyed it.

So Aoki founded Blue Tree Hotels in 1997—*aoki* means "blue tree" in Japanese. What makes her luxury hotels different from others is that they combine Japanese attention to detail with Brazilian warmth. Blue Tree Hotels is now one of the largest hotel chains in Brazil, and in 2013 Aoki was named the second most powerful businesswoman in the country.

At the age of eight, Divyank Turakhia found his niche when he began teaching himself computer programming. By 1995, public internet access came to his hometown of Mumbai, India, and he had enough experience to build websites for companies. Although he was only 13, he also did web consulting and answered internet-security questions.

In 1998 Turakhia and his older brother, Bhavin, asked their dad for a $500 loan to launch a web-hosting business, Directi. The boys were only 16 and 18. It wasn't a small amount of money for the family, but their dad had seen how hard the brothers were already working in the tech field. And he said something that has always stuck with Turakhia: "If you want to try something, try anything, it's okay to fail."

But the boys succeeded. By the time Turakhia was 18, he had made his first million dollars—he had clearly found the right business for him. He has since branched out many times from Directi. In 2005 he started the

company Skenzo to buy unused web domains and sell them. Five years later Turakhia turned that business into Media.net to get into the online advertising field. He sold that company in 2016 for almost a billion dollars!

The great thing about an entrepreneur finding the right work is the satisfaction it brings. "Am I happy? Yeah, absolutely," says Turakhia. "If I wasn't happy I wouldn't do it."

Buying and selling web domains is just one of the many businesses that Divyank Turakhia's love of computer technology has led him to create.

"When you're an entrepreneur, you have to go in feeling like you're going to be successful."

—Lillian Vernon, founder of Lillian Vernon Corp.

GETTING THE RIGHT JOB

Oprah Winfrey
(1954–)

GREAT IDEA!

Where to Get Ideas to Become an Entrepreneur

Want to become an entrepreneur but don't know how to start? Go through your day from start to finish and look for a situation or problem, no matter how small, that could be improved or solved. What service or invention could make life better?

Or are there chores someone would pay you to do? Can you build a business around them? Pick the thing you're best at and that interests you enough to work hard at it. You can find tips about becoming an entrepreneur online and in books.

Oprah Winfrey started in television as a news anchor in 1973 at a station in Nashville. Three years later she was a co-anchor in Baltimore. But Winfrey found she couldn't just be a reporter. She got involved in the stories and was more concerned about the people than the news. That ended up getting her fired.

Winfrey was given another job co-hosting a talk show. It wasn't as high-profile as the previous job, but Winfrey loved it. She found she could talk easily to anyone, say what she thought and interact with the audience.

Winfrey had always wanted to work in Chicago, and in 1984 she was offered the job of hosting a little-watched, 30-minute talk show there. Because of Winfrey's empathy, enthusiasm and talent, in just months the show went from last place in the market to the top-rated talk show in Chicago. It was expanded to an hour and renamed *The Oprah Winfrey Show*. In 1986 the program went national. The show was the highest-rated TV production of its type and ran until 2001.

Winfrey has also written books and starred in movies. She publishes *O, the Oprah Magazine* and has a radio channel. No wonder she was North America's first Black multibillionaire.

Winfrey has been rated the greatest Black American **philanthropist** ever. Her special focus is women and children in need—in 2007 she donated $40 million to open a school for gifted girls in Africa.

> **"I don't believe in failure. It is not failure if you enjoyed the process."**
> —Oprah Winfrey,
> media entrepreneur

Oprah Winfrey is one of the most famous entrepreneurs and philanthropists ever. She motivates people around the world.

WETTER IS BETTER

Lonnie Johnson
(1949–)

SUCCESS!

HIGH-FLYING ENTREPRENEUR

An African trip turned Teara Fraser into an entrepreneur. She saw how amazing the land looked from the air and decided to become a pilot. In October 2019 Fraser launched Iskwew Air—*iskwew* (pronounced iss-kway-yo) is Cree for "woman"—to serve communities throughout British Columbia.

As owner of the first female-run, Indigenous airline, Fraser supports Indigenous tourism and other female and Indigenous entrepreneurs. In 2021 this Métis businesswoman of Cree ancestry was included in *Wonderful Women of History*, a DC Comics graphic novel.

Whoosh! The Super Soaker water gun is one of the world's bestselling toys. But when Lonnie Johnson invented it, it was just something he'd been tinkering with in his spare time.

Johnson had been interested in science since he was a kid. In high school he was the only Black student to take part in a science fair in his home state of Alabama. Johnson's robot powered by compressed air won him first prize.

At university Johnson studied engineering. He worked for the United States Air Force, then joined the jet propulsion laboratory at the National Aeronautics and Space Administration (NASA) in 1979. He worked on many projects, including developing the nuclear power source for the Galileo mission to Jupiter.

But at home one weekend in 1982, Johnson was working on a cooling device that ran on water. He hooked up the vinyl tubing at one end of his invention to the bathroom faucet. When he pumped the nozzle at the other end, a blast of water shot out! "Jeez, this would

Kids enjoy wet summer fun with Lonnie Johnson's incredible Super Soaker toy.

make a great water gun," Johnson said to himself. It was powered by compressed air, just like his robot of many years before.

It took Johnson years to perfect the Super Soaker. But since it started selling, people around the world have bought about 200 million of these amazing squirt guns, totaling nearly $1 billion in sales. This huge success meant Johnson could keep inventing. In 1991 he founded Johnson Research and Development Co., Inc., and he now holds more than 100 patents. This accidental entrepreneur also started an organization to encourage kids to enjoy math and science.

"Pursue your dreams!"

—Rachel A. Olsen, motivational author

CHAPTER NINE
STICK TO IT

Becoming an entrepreneur at any age is challenging, but it can be especially difficult if you're a kid. As a kid you don't have a lot of experience or education. But young entrepreneurs like Sreelakshmi Suresh prove that determination, hard work and clear goals can make an entrepreneur successful at any age.

Suresh, from Kozhikode, India, began using the computer at age three. She learned the English alphabet by typing on the computer. She drew pictures using the computer. When she was six, her father showed her a website a young boy had designed and encouraged Suresh to make a website herself. Soon after, that's just what she did.

Suresh was especially fascinated by **logos**. One of the websites and logos she created attracts visitors to her home state, beautiful Kerala. "I have to be the master of my field," she says. "I have to work hard and study more and more to achieve this." And she believes in kidpreneurs. "Don't think that something is impossible for children. We can achieve whatever elders can do, if we have the will. Keep moving. Don't quit is my motto."

> **"Winners never quit, and quitters never win."**
>
> —Vince Lombardi, former NFL football coach, described as one of the best in the league's history

Penny Streeter of South Africa knows about persisting even when times are tough. More than 25 years ago, the former **beautician** was a broke and pregnant single mom. Streeter and her family had to live in temporary accommodations. It was devastating. Her business had failed, and she had debts she couldn't pay.

But Streeter took a deep breath and started again, working as a children's entertainer to help get the money to open a new business recruiting nursing staff. This business was successful, and Streeter expanded into owning a golf club and a winery. She is now one of the richest women in South Africa.

WALK TALL

Amit Goffer

(1953–)

It started in 1996 with an unexpected win. Lily Goffer, the wife of Amit Goffer, the Israeli chief executive officer of a successful company that made **MRI (magnetic resonance imaging)** machines for operating rooms, filled out a form to win an all-terrain vehicle (ATV). When she won, her husband, who wasn't interested in the vehicle, sold it to a neighbor. His kids were so disappointed that Goffer agreed to rent a few ATVs for a ride in the Israeli wilderness.

To their shock, soon after Goffer set off in one of the vehicles with his daughter, they flew off the trail and hit a tree. Goffer's daughter was unhurt, but Goffer's neck was broken. "I couldn't feel anything," he said, "and I knew immediately what had happened to me." Goffer was a **quadriplegic** and would never walk again.

After months of pain and disorientation caused by his debilitating condition, Goffer began to look for a way to become independent again. He didn't want to live his life in a wheelchair and was determined to find an alternative. That will to change his circumstances and help others in similar situations led to the creation of ReWalk, a device that helps people with spinal cord injuries stand, walk, turn and go up and down stairs.

SUCCESS!

CHANGING DIRECTIONS

When Partha Unnava broke his ankle and spent weeks on uncomfortable crutches, he knew there was a need for more-comfortable crutches. So he started Better Walk, a company and product that earned him entrepreneurship awards, a meeting with former president Barack Obama and recognition by *Forbes* magazine.

When Unnava ran into difficulties selling his product, he changed direction and created Lasso, a company that sells socks that reduce the risk of ankle injury.

ReWalk was tested for the first time by disabled volunteers on Goffer's driveway. To everyone's joy, it worked! Although it took a few more years for ReWalk to become accepted and recognized, Goffer persisted.

Sadly, the one person who couldn't benefit was Goffer himself. His injuries were too severe. But Goffer didn't give up. The company he co-founded developed a new device called UPnRIDE, and with it Goffer was able to stand for the first time in 18 years. In 2020, UPnRIDE was approved by the Food and Drug Administration (FDA) in the United States. Soon more people will have the chance to walk again—or for the first time.

"If you start thinking you are good at something, that's often the day you stop trying to be better."
—Drew Houston, co-founder and chief executive officer of Dropbox

Amit Goffer's products change lives and give many people the gift of walking.

NOTHING STOPPED HER

Madam C.J. Walker
(1867–1919)

"I'm convinced that about half of what separates the successful entrepreneurs from the nonsuccessful ones is pure perseverance."

—Steve Jobs, co-founder of Apple Inc.

Sarah Breedlove was born on a **plantation** in Louisiana. Her parents were former slaves. She was orphaned at seven and a widow and mother at 20. Determined to give her young daughter a better life, Breedlove moved to St. Louis and worked as a washerwoman and a cook.

It was a hard life, made worse by poor living conditions and little access to clean water. When Breedlove began to lose her hair, she looked for a way to help not only herself but other Black women living in poverty. She experimented with different hair products that were said to help with baldness and worked as a sales agent for the founder of a hair-product company.

As time went on, Breedlove wanted to be her own boss and develop her own hair products. In 1906 she married salesman Charles J. Walker, began calling herself Madam C.J. Walker and started her own business.

In those days there were few opportunities for Black women, especially in the South, but nothing stopped Walker. She learned how to market and sell her hair

products and promoted **hygiene** and beauty. She trained other women to sell her products. "I am not merely satisfied in making money for myself," she said in 1914. "I am endeavoring to provide employment for hundreds of women of my race." She also expanded her business and sold her products in other countries.

Walker not only became one of the first Black millionaire businesswomen but also empowered others to become successful entrepreneurs. She gave back to her community. She stood up against **lynching**. She provided scholarships for students at Black colleges, supported orphanages and retirement homes and advocated for Black soldiers who served in World War I.

Madam C.J. Walker not only became a successful entrepreneur but also promoted art, theater and education.

"One of the greatest skills of leadership is being unflappable. Anytime you do anything in the world, there's going to be criticism."

—Arianna Huffington, businessperson, writer and co-founder of the *Huffington Post* (now *HuffPost*)

FEEDING EVERYONE

José Andrés
(1969–)

Growing up in Spain, José Andrés loved the smell, the feel and the taste of food, especially when it was cooked right on the fire.

Andrés attended cooking school in Barcelona and briefly worked for a Spanish admiral at sea. He then headed to New York City in 1991 with only $50 in his pocket. Soon after he arrived, he began watching the famous chef Julia Child on TV. "I was fascinated by the way she would express herself," he says. "The way she will make you feel like that one chicken she had in front of her was the most important thing in the history of mankind."

Andrés praised other chefs who influenced his cooking and restaurant skills, such as Ferran Adrià and Jean-Louis Neichel. He opened a successful tapas restaurant, serving small-plate Spanish food, in Washington, DC. His restaurant success grew swiftly, and he expanded into California, Nevada and other areas.

In 2010, after a devastating earthquake hit Haiti, Andrés created a mobile food-relief program called

"I find it best to dive right in and learn the hard way."

—Pete Cashmore, founder of Mashable

World Central Kitchen. When a hurricane hit Puerto Rico, Andrés and his organization hurried to provide food and relief, serving almost 400,000 hot meals on the island. Andrés has skillfully managed to continue growing his successful restaurant business while providing food relief in disasters.

In 2019 the Julia Child Foundation honored Andrés's public spirit, cooking expertise and mentorship of others. He continued his restaurant business while helping the hungry during the COVID-19 pandemic. By the start of 2021, World Central Kitchen provided more than 35 million meals across the United States.

GREAT IDEA!

The Restaurant Business

Opening a restaurant is not easy. Sixty percent of restaurants don't make it past their first year, and 80 percent go out of business within five years. But some restaurants are successful. Ones that do well hire a good chef and competent staff, find the right location, get the word out about their business and give customers value for their money.

Chef José Andrés and US vice president Kamala Harris exchange greetings during tough COVID times.

VICTORIA KISYOMBE

Kalsoom Lakhani

BILL GATES

CHAPTER TEN
ALWAYS BE LEARNING

Anna Wright is an Australian entrepreneur who developed the mobile app BindiMaps to let visually impaired people know where **braille** signs are. She came up with the idea after helping other people start companies and learning from those experiences.

Wright has had numerous surgeries to save her vision and knows the importance of being able to locate braille signs. BindiMaps, launched in 2017, uses a network of Bluetooth beacons that combine with an audio system to tell visually impaired people where they are and help them move around safely.

Finding answers is just one thing entrepreneurs are good at. They ask questions, figure out what they don't know, then get education or experience. They listen to customers and employees to discover what's important to them, what they need and why.

In 2011, when one of Dan Price's employees at Gravity Payments told him he wasn't paying his staff enough, Price listened and learned. Now his employees each earn at least $70,000, and Price took a $1 million pay cut. The raises energized Price's employees, and Gravity became much more successful.

Price became an accidental entrepreneur at 16 when his rock band broke up. He'd been playing in bars and coffee shops and saw the high rates owners paid to companies that process credit-card transactions. Gravity, based in Seattle, offers clients better service and charges lower prices than its competitors. During the COVID-19 pandemic, employees offered to take major pay cuts to keep the company going.

GREAT IDEA!

Printing Possibilities

In 2014, 12-year-old Shubham Banerjee from Santa Clara, California, needed an idea for a science-fair project. He'd read how technology can really help visually impaired people. So Banerjee decided to create an inexpensive braille printer to print pages of the raised dots that blind people read by touch.

Using a Lego robotics kit and electrical components, Banerjee created the Braigo printer—the name combines *braille* and *Lego*.

WARRIOR WOMEN AND EVERYDAY HEROES

Kalsoom Lakhani
(1982–)

"Trying and failing isn't something to avoid. Fail fast and learn faster."

—Nick Mares,
co-founder of Kettle & Fire

Learning for Kalsoom Lakhani started with her family. "I grew up on stories of the warrior women on my mother's side of the family, and my grandmother was often the larger-than-life central character," says Lakhani. "I hope I keep her spirit alive by pursuing my own goals with the same passion and determination."

Lakhani was raised in Dhaka, Bangladesh, and Islamabad, Pakistan, but she attended university in the United States, where she took classes in foreign affairs and Middle East Studies.

In 2011 Lakhani started Invest2Innovate (i2i) Ventures to support start-up businesses in Pakistan. The company trains and encourages budding entrepreneurs. For instance, doctHERs uses technology to connect

out-of-work Pakistani female doctors with patients. The Reading Room Project creates learning environments for students with low incomes. i2i Ventures also connects start-up companies with investors and provides information such as market opportunities and start-up growth rates.

Since Lakhani began her company, she has trained businesspeople in several countries, including Cambodia, Ireland, Nepal and Ukraine. She especially likes to encourage women to start businesses. "For women entrepreneurs specifically, don't let anyone put you in a box, because people will do that constantly," Lakhani advises. "Focus on putting your head down and executing on your business."

Lakhani gives back to the people of Pakistan through The Hero Project, which she co-founded to celebrate everyday heroes. As well, from 2008 to 2011 she was the director of Social Vision, which provides funding for innovative organizations just getting started.

Pakistan has provided many opportunities for Kalsoom Lakhani to start and support businesses. She's motivated by her desire to improve and learn.

SUCCESS!

MIGHTY MASKS

University student Joshua Sofer's summer internship in 2020 was canceled because of COVID-19. Rather than look for another job, he and his friend Matthew Danics decided to start their own company.

Canadian Face Masks not only sells face masks at competitive prices, but also provided other students with work and practical experience when many of their summer jobs were canceled. For every 10 organic masks the Toronto-based firm sells, it donates one to local volunteer organizations.

SOFTWARE GENIUS

Bill Gates
(1955–)

GREAT IDEA!

Just Get Started

Don't wait to become an entrepreneur until you've got the perfect idea. Just begin—you can learn and improve your business as you go.

It's great to get feedback on your company, but you can't make everyone happy. Come up with an idea for a product or service that you'd pay to use. Make it something *you* love, rather than guessing at what others like. Don't worry too much about the competition at first. Focus on your business and how to make it great!

Even as a kid growing up in Seattle, Bill Gates loved learning—he read the encyclopedia for fun. In 1968, when Gates was 13, he wrote his first software program—it was for a tic-tac-toe game. Soon he was dreaming of "a world in which machines would do all the boring parts of work and people would be free to be creative and productive." About a year later, he and a school friend, Paul Allen, were both working for a local company, finding the bugs in its new computer system.

When Gates was 15, he and Allen were hired by a company doing work for the US government's defense department. With every job, Gates learned more about programming, and he and Allen started their own company, counting traffic for cities. But the business failed—one reason was that people discovered it was run by teenagers.

In 1973 Gates started college, but while there he and Allen were still working on software. In 1975 the pair formed another company. They combined the words *microcomputer* and *software* to create the name Microsoft. Gates quit university to focus on his business.

Today Microsoft is the world's largest computer software company, and Gates is one of the richest people in the world. He and his former wife, Melinda, set up the Bill & Melinda Gates Foundation in 2000 to improve education and public health around the world. Since then they've given more than $50 billion to charities. Now Gates works hard at learning the best ways to spend his money helping people.

"What I learn from talking to so many women around the world: If you can empower them with the right things, the right tools, they can lift up their family. And that ultimately lifts up their community and their society."

—Melinda Gates,
philanthropist

The Bill & Melinda Gates Foundation is the second-largest charitable foundation in the world. One of its goals is to reduce extreme poverty around the world.

THE COMPANY NAMED AFTER A COW

Victoria Kisyombe
(c. 1957–)

SUCCESS!

COFFEE BREAK

Mark Marsolais-Nahwegahbow is Ojibwe and a band member of Ontario's Whitefish River First Nation. He studied to be a **correctional worker** and worked in the criminal justice system, focusing on helping Indigenous people. In 2018 Marsolais-Nahwegahbow founded Birch Bark Coffee Company as another way of assisting people.

The company uses organic beans from Indigenous farmers in Central and South America. Marsolais-Nahwegahbow uses some of the money from coffee sales to buy water purifiers for Indigenous families across Canada.

When Victoria Kisyombe's husband died, she had three young children to care for. This veterinarian quickly discovered that she couldn't earn enough to pay her family's bills. What could she do?

Luckily, the Tanzanian family had a cow named Sero (the word means "leader" in the Maasai language) that produced enough milk for the family to drink and sell. Kisyombe thought about how important the cow was to the family and how many women don't have a similar way to make money.

Kisyombe learned from the experience. In 2002 she started a company to help other women, even though she had no training in business. Kisyombe bought equipment that clients needed but couldn't afford to purchase and then leased (a type of rental) it to them.

The leases have included fridges and freezers for convenience stores, sewing machines, water pumps for

irrigation, and farm tools. Kisyombe called her company SELFINA, which stands for Sero Lease and Finance Ltd. How many cows have a company named after them?

The business was a success. The cost of the leases is low—they're called **micro-leases**—which means very few women are unable to pay them.

Since SELFINA started, more than 27,000 women have leased equipment, 150 jobs have been created, and the company has had an impact on the lives of more than 250,000 entrepreneurs, family members and others. To further help women entrepreneurs, Kisyombe started SEBA (Sero Businesswomen Association). It's a nonprofit group that empowers women entrepreneurs.

Victoria Kisyombe (front center) aims to empower women through entrepreneurship seminars.

"I learned to always take on things I'd never done before. Growth and comfort do not coexist."

—Virginia Rometty,
former chief executive officer of IBM

So you want to be an accidental entrepreneur?

1. **BE OPEN TO RISK**: Successful entrepreneurs are open to taking risks and changing direction when needed.

2. **SEIZE OPPORTUNITIES**: Grab chances when you see them, whether it's a service that doesn't exist or a product you think could change the world. Be ready to change direction and try new ideas.

3. **DO WHAT YOU DO BEST**: Use your skills and follow your passion when starting a business. That will help you keep your business going even when times get tough.

4. **DON'T WORRY THAT YOU'RE TOO OLD OR TOO YOUNG**: Don't let your age make you feel you can't start a business or create a great new product. Passion and enthusiasm will help you overcome many obstacles!

5. **TAKE ADVICE FROM PEOPLE YOU ADMIRE**: Wise entrepreneurs learn from the successes and failures of others. They ask for advice and listen to good ideas.

6. **BE A PLANNER**: Think ahead, notice trends in the market and be flexible. Good businesses thrive with thoughtful preparation and planning.

7. **GO GREEN**: Caring for the environment is not only a good way to help the planet but can also lead to a successful business. It's great when your product or service can make the world a better place.

8. **FIND YOUR NICHE**: Discover what you love to do and then do it well. Solve problems and innovate to make a product or service unlike any other.

9. **STICK TO IT**: Hard work, clear goals and persistence pay off in running a business through good times and challenging times. Never give up!

10. **ALWAYS BE LEARNING**: Be curious. Listen to customers to learn what's important to them. Ask questions, find answers and get educated.

GLOSSARY

analytics—the analysis of data using computer software

app—short for *application*, a specialized computer program on a smartphone or other electronice device

beautician—a person who provides hairstyling, manicures and other beauty treatments

biodegradable—capable of being broken down by living organisms such as bacteria

biodiversity—the variety of plant and animal species in an environment

biotechnology—the use of living organisms to make useful chemicals or products in agriculture, food science and medicine

braille—a system of writing and printing for people with visual disabilities in which raised dots represent letters and numbers that can be "read" with the fingers

brand—the name, symbol or other feature that distinguishes one seller's products or services from another's

code—(verb) to write programming language, or code, that tells a computer to do a specific task

collaborated—worked together

concentration camps—places like those built by the Nazis during World War II where Jews, political prisoners and others were persecuted, tortured and killed

correctional worker—a person who enforces rules, keeps order and supervises inmates in a jail

correspondence course—a course of study where students and teachers communicate by email

deforestation—the action of clearing or cutting down forests without replanting trees

dengue fever—a serious tropical disease, transmitted by mosquitoes, that causes headache, severe joint pain, high fever and other symptoms

discount—a reduction in the usual price of something

discrimination—unjust treatment of people based on characteristics such as their skin color, gender or age

erosion—the wearing away of rock and soil by gravity, ice, water or wind

fax machines—devices that send, receive, copy and print documents using telephone equipment

foot-and-mouth disease—a highly contagious disease that affects and sometimes kills cloven-hoofed animals (animals with a hoof split into two toes, such as sheep and cattle)

franchise—the right to sell a company's goods or services in a particular area

hygiene—the conditions or practices that contribute to good health, such as bathing and brushing one's teeth

intern—someone who works at a paid or unpaid job that gives them practical experience in a particular field of work

lab technician—a skilled worker who does a variety of jobs in a laboratory, a room equipped to conduct research

logo—the graphic trademark or symbol identifying a company or product

lynching—the unfair killing of someone, usually by hanging, through mob action, with no trial or legal approval

marginalized—treated as unimportant or powerless

marketing—promotion and advertising to encourage people to buy a product or service

media—means of communication, such as newspapers, magazines, TV, internet, etc., designed to reach masses of people

micro-lease—a low lease or rental fee on equipment that allows an entrepreneur to build a small business

mobile—able to move freely or easily. The term is also used to describe phones, computers and similar devices.

MRI (magnetic resonance imaging)—magnetic resonance imaging, a method of getting detailed images of organs and tissues inside the body

NASA (National Aeronautics and Space Administration)—a United States agency that runs space programs and conducts space-related research

nonprofit—(noun) a group or company that does not conduct business in order to make a profit from their work but to help people

nuclear disarmament—the act of reducing or eliminating nuclear weapons, the most dangerous weapons on Earth

organic waste—any material that is biodegradable and comes from a plant or animal; includes food scraps, paper towels and leaves

pandemic—an outbreak of a disease that attacks a large population and occurs in a whole country or much of the world

patent—an official document that gives an inventor the right to exclude others from making or selling their invention

philanthropist—a person who donates goods, money or time to help others

pinball machines—devices for playing pinball, a game in which a player shoots a ball down a sloping table that has obstacles and targets with scores, which are automatically recorded when the ball hits them

plantation—a large farm or estate, usually in a hot climate, where crops like cotton, sugar or tea are grown

programmer—a person who writes the instructions that run computer programs

quadriplegic—someone whose arms and legs are partially or completely paralyzed (unable to move) due to an injury or disease

renewable resource—a resource that can be used repeatedly and doesn't run out. Two examples are solar and wind energy.

scholarship—money granted to a student to support their education

social services—government services that help people with such needs as education, health and housing

software developer—someone who designs computer apps and software programs and oversees their production

solar power—energy from the sun converted into electricity

stocks—shares in the ownership of a company that are bought and sold. Investors buy stocks hoping they will go up in value.

RESOURCES

PRINT

Andal, Walter. *Finance 101 for Kids: Money Lessons Children Cannot Afford to Miss.* Maitland, FL: Mill City Press, Inc., 2016.

Bridges, Moziah. *Mo's Bows: A Young Person's Guide to Start-Up Success.* New York: Running Press Kids, 2019.

Bryant, Jill. *Phenomenal Female Entrepreneurs.* Toronto: Second Story Press, 2013.

Cuban, Mark, Shaan Patel and Ian McCue. *Kid Start-Up: How YOU Can Become an Entrepreneur.* New York: Diversion Books, 2018.

Kravetz, Stacy. *She's So Boss: The Girl Entrepreneur's Guide to Imagining, Creating & Kicking Ass.* London, UK: Quercus Books, 2017.

Lager, Fred. *Ben & Jerry's: The Inside Scoop: How Two Real Guys Built a Business with a Social Conscience and a Sense of Humor.* New York: Crown, 1995.

Larsen, Andrew. *The Man Who Loved Libraries: The Story of Andrew Carnegie.* Toronto: Owlkids, 2017.

Lobb, Nancy. *16 Extraordinary American Entrepreneurs.* Portland, ME: J. Weston Walch Publisher, 2008.

Mariotti, Steve. *The Young Entrepreneur's Guide to Starting and Running a Business: Turn Your Ideas into Money!* New York: Crown Business, 2014.

McLuskey, Krista. *Entrepreneurs* (Women in Profile). St. Catharines, ON: Crabtree Publishing, 1998.

Merberg, Julie, and Sarah Parvis. *How to Start Your Very First Business.* New York: Downtown Bookworks, 2015.

Nichols, Catherine. *Madam C.J. Walker.* New York: Children's Press, 2005.

Penn, Maya S. *You Got This! Unleash Your Awesomeness, Find Your Path, and Change Your World.* New York: Gallery Books, 2016.

Rebel Girls. *Madam C.J. Walker Builds a Business.* Los Angeles: Rebel Girls, 2019.

Spencer, Mick. *Start Before You're Ready: The Young Entrepreneur's Guide to Extraordinary Success in Work and Life.* Hoboken, NJ: John Wiley & Sons, Inc., 2019.

Spinner, Stephanie. *Who Is Steven Spielberg?* New York: Penguin Workshop, 2013.

Toren, Adam, and Matthew Toren. *Kidpreneurs: Young Entrepreneurs with Big Ideas!* Phoenix, AZ: Business Plus Media Group LLC, 2009.

Turner, Ted. *Call Me Ted.* New York: Grand Central Publishing, 2008.

FILM

D'Auria, Michele, dir. *Sōichirō Honda: The Power of Dreams.* 2011; Rome: Honda Italia Industriale S.p.A.

Guggenheim, Davis, dir. *Inside Bill's Brain: Decoding Bill Gates.* 2019; Los Gatos, CA: Netflix.

Guss, Alison, and Greg Weinstein, writ. *Colonel Sanders: America's Chicken King.* 1998; New York: A+E Networks.

Kunhardt, Peter W, dir. *Becoming Warren Buffet.* 2017; HBO.

McGregor, Kristen, and Jennifer Treuting, dir. *Mo's Bows.* 2015; Brooklyn: Squirrel Friends TV.

ONLINE

Acton Children's Business Fair: childrensbusinessfair.org
Alex "Nemo" Hanse: thefoolies.com
Amar Bose: bose.ca
Andrew Cooper and Alex Schulze: 4ocean.com
Anita Roddick: thebodyshop.com
Anna Wright: bindimaps.com
Anneke van den Broek: rufusandcoco.com
Arlene Dickinson: arlenedickinson.com
Ben & Jerry's: benandjerrys.ca/en/about-us
Ben Stern: nohbo.com
Bill Gates: gatesfoundation.org
Dan Price: gravitypayments.com
Frederick Jones: biography.com/inventor/frederick-jones
Futurpreneur: futurpreneur.ca
José Andrés: joseandres.com
Kalsoom Lakhani: invest2innovate.com
Lynda Kemp: thunderthighscostumes.com
Lynn-Marie and Melissa-Rae Angus: sisterssage.com
Madelyn Rich: accentsbym.com
Mark Marsolais-Nahwegahbow: birchbarkcoffeecompany.com
Maya Penn: mayasideas.com
Mira Modi: dicewarepasswords.com
Moziah Bridges: mosbowsmemphis.com
Natasha Rufus Isaacs and Lavinia Brennan: beulahlondon.com
Oprah Winfrey: oprah.com
REMAKEHUB: remakehub.co
Sara Blakely: spanx.com/about-us
Shubham Banerjee: shu.today
Steven Spielberg: spielbergfilmarchive.org.il
Ted Turner: tedturner.com
Victoria Kisyombe: selfina.com
Warren Buffet: biography.com/business-figure/warren-buffett

Links to external resources are for personal and/or educational use only and are provided in good faith without any express or implied warranty. There is no guarantee given as to the accuracy or currency of any individual item. The authors and publisher provide links as a service to readers. This does not imply any endorsement by the authors or publisher of any of the content accessed through these links.

INDEX

Page numbers in **bold** indicate an image caption.

PHOTO CREDITS

CHAPTER ONE: p.2 (collage): Nataliia Pyzhova/Shutterstock.com; Keith Homan/Shutterstock.com; Mike Windle/Getty Images; JHVEPhoto/Shutterstock.com; courtesy of Fariel Salahuddin. **Ben Cohen and Jerry Greenfield:** p. 4 Featureflash Photo Agency/Shutterstock.com; p. 5 (and collage) Chip Somodevilla/Getty Images. **Sara Blakely:** p. 6 Laurence Agron/Dreamstime.com; p. 7 Ken Wolter/Dreamstime.com. **Fariel Salahuddin:** pp. 8 and 9 courtesy of Fariel Salahuddin.

CHAPTER TWO: p. 10 (collage): courtesy of Lynn-Marie Angus; Rawpixel.com/Shutterstock.com. **Lynn-Marie and Melissa-Rae Angus:** pp. 12 and 13 courtesy of Lynn-Marie Angus. **Alex "Nemo" Hanse:** pp. 14 and 15 (and collage) Alex Nemo Hanse/Unsplash. **Mira Modi:** p. 16 (and collage) Ozornina Kseniia/Shutterstock.com; p. 17 wera Rodsawang/Getty Images.

CHAPTER THREE: p. 18 (collage): Nadezhda Bolotina/Shutterstock.com; andyparker72/Shutterstock.com; from the family archives of Lynda Kemp, edited by James Robert Durant; Rosana Khabbaz, designer and model: Amanda Fielding; FOTOGRIN/Shutterstock.com; Luis Molinero/Shutterstock.com; Jag_cz/Shutterstock.com. **Warren Buffett:** p. 20 David Silverman/Getty Images; p. 21 (and collage) Mario Tama/Getty Images. **Frederick McKinley Jones:** pp. 22 and 23 (and collage) ©Thermo King. **Lynda Kemp:** pp. 24 and 25 from the family archives of Lynda Kemp, edited by James Robert Durant.

CHAPTER FOUR: p. 26 (collage): Bacharz/Shutterstock.com; Oleksiy Mark/Shutterstock.com. **Chen Yuheng:** p. 29 hugo_34/Shutterstock.com. **Harbhajan Kaur:** pp. 30 and 31 (and collage) courtesy of Harbhajan Kaur. **Moziah Bridges:** p. 32 Craig Barritt/Getty Images; p. 33 (and collage) Jerritt Clark/Getty Images.

CHAPTER FIVE: p. 34 (collage): AlinaMD/Shutterstock.com; DFree/Shutterstock.com; Pavel L Photo and Video/Shutterstock.com; New Africa/Shutterstock.com; Gregory James Van Raalte/Shutterstock.com. **Asia Newson:** pp. 36 and 37 (and collage) courtesy of LaTasha Thomas. **Steven Spielberg:** p. 38 Rich Fury/Getty Images; p. 39 Kevin Winter/Getty Images. **Martin Radtke:** p. 40 Peter Kaminski/Flickr.com (CC BY 2.0); p. 41 Stephanie Keith/Getty Images.

CHAPTER SIX: p. 42 (collage): Kathy Hutchins/Shutterstock.com; Tami Freed/Shutterstock.com; LouiesWorld1/Shutterstock.com; Random NZ Photography/Shutterstock.com; SGM/Shutterstock.com; Jonathan Weiss/Shutterstock.com; Bruno Vincent/Getty Images; Anetam/Shutterstock.com. **Ted Turner:** p. 44 Ben Rose/Getty Images; p. 45 Alex Wong/Getty Images. **Amar Bose:** p. 46 (and collage) Janet Knott/Boston Globe/Getty Images; p. 47 DCStockPhotography/Shutterstock.com. **Anita Roddick:** p. 48 Chris Jackson/Getty Images; p. 49 Ian Gavan/Getty Images.

CHAPTER SEVEN: p. 50 (collage): Elzoy/Shutterstock.com; hyotographics/Shutterstock.com; REMAKEHUB; 4ocean; frank60/Shutterstock.com. **Jean Bosco Nzeyimana:** pp. 52 and 53 (and collage) Justin Sullivan/Getty Images. **Sissi Chao:** p. 54 (top and bottom; and collage) REMAKEHUB; p. 55 courtesy of Sissi Chao/REMAKEHUB. **Andrew Cooper and Alex Schulze:** pp. 56 and 57 4ocean.

CHAPTER EIGHT: p. 58 (collage): Alexander Supertramp/Shutterstock.com; sbukley/Shutterstock.com; cigdern/Shutterstock.com; BokehStore/Shutterstock.com; Jamie Lamor Thompson/Shutterstock.com; urbanbuzz/Shutterstock.com. **Divyank Turakhia:** p. 60 (and collage) Wikimedia Commons/Aviefern (CC BY-SA 4.0); p. 61 Tetra Images/Getty Images. **Oprah Winfrey:** p. 62 Getty Images; p. 63 Emma McIntyre/Getty Images. **Lonnie Johnson:** p. 64 Wikimedia Commons/Office of Naval Research (Public Domain); p. 65 LEE SNIDER PHOTO IMAGES/Shutterstock.com.

CHAPTER NINE: p. 66 (collage): Madam Walker family archives/A'Lelia Bundles; courtesy of World Central Kitchen; Larry French/Getty Images. **Amit Goffer:** p. 68 (and collage) Sean Dempsey/Alamy Stock Photo; p. 69 (and collage) Peter Macdiarmid/Getty Images. **Madam C.J. Walker:** pp. 70 and 71 (and collage) Madam Walker family archives/A'Lelia Bundles. **José Andrés:** p. 72 Shannon Finney/Getty Images; p. 73 Alex Wong/Getty Images.

CHAPTER TEN: p. 74 (collage): Frederic Legrand - COMEO/Shutterstock.com; JeanLucIchard/Shutterstock.com; Ga Stock/Shutterstock.com. **Kalsoom Lakhani:** p. 77 Almas Afzal/500px/Getty Images. **Bill Gates:** p. 78 Getty Images; p. 79 David Ryder/Getty Images. **Victoria Kisyombe:** pp. 80 and 81 courtesy of Dr. Victoria Kisyombe/SELFINA; pp. 82 and 83 FreshSplash/Getty Images.

Every effort has been made to locate and credit the correct copyright owners of the images used in this book.
The publisher apologizes for any errors or omissions and would be grateful if notified of corrections
that should be made in future reprints or editions.

ACKNOWLEDGMENTS

We loved working on another book with our great editor, Kirstie Hudson, and illustrator Jenn Playford. Many thanks as well to designer Rachel Page and copy editor Vivian Sinclair. We're also very grateful to Andrew Wooldridge and Ruth Linka of Orca Book Publishers for publishing this series.

Liz says: Many thanks to Frieda for joining me on another co-writing adventure. We both appreciate the entrepreneurs who responded to our questions and provided photographs. Thanks also to Amy Demoulin, Raphael Arens and Jonah Arens for their support of this book. Special thanks always to John and Douglas. And very special thanks to Paul, who makes the business of being married simply lovely!

Frieda says: It's been fascinating to discover the stories of so many amazing entrepreneurs who not only had successful businesses but also used that success to help others. Thanks as always to Liz MacLeod for another wonderful book journey. Here's to more! Special thanks to Philippa Dowding, Michele Landsberg, Ken Setterington, Maria Martella, Donald Loggins and Emma and Steve Biggs for sharing their stories of people we profiled. I'm grateful to Bill and David Wishinsky for their support and conversations. They've sparked great ideas.

ABOUT THE AUTHORS

Elizabeth MacLeod especially enjoyed researching and writing about the ecopreneurs in this book—see chapter 7. She hopes these stories will inspire readers to fight climate change. Liz has written more than 70 biographies, picture books, cookbooks and other nonfiction books. She's won many awards for her work, including Children's Choice awards across Canada and the Norma Fleck Award for Canadian Children's Non-Fiction. This is the sixth book Liz and Frieda have written together—their most recent are *How to Become an Accidental Activist* and *How to Become an Accidental Genius*.

Frieda Wishinsky loves discovering stories. She's an international award-winning author of over 70 books, from picture books to chapter books to novels and nonfiction. She's also a freelance editor who enjoys helping other writers write great stories. Frieda loves gardens and gardening, traveling, hiking and finding new ideas in books, movies, conversations and trips.

DON'T ACCIDENTALLY MISS OUT!

Don't be afraid to try! Make connections! Be persistent! Ask questions!

Get started! Be unstoppable! Dream big to change the world!

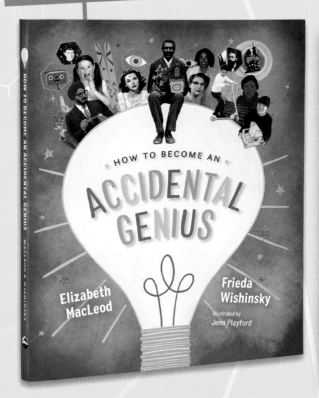

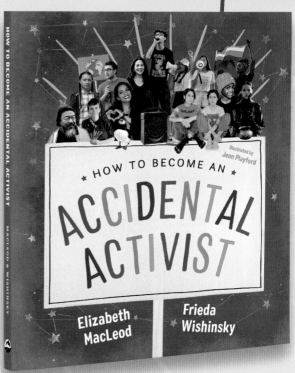

LEARN THE SECRETS AND AMAZING STORIES OF SUCCESSFUL INVENTORS

PROFILES OF ALMOST 100 ACTIVISTS FROM AROUND THE WORLD

★"A treasure trove of inspirational people and ideas."
—*Canadian Children's Book News*

"Will inspire readers."
—*School Library Journal*